Depression

essence, meaning, support, treatment

by

Valentin Boyadzhiev
psychologist, dietologist, psychoanalyst in
formation
member of ISAP, ІАНТ, АБПП

Contents:

Introduction

Ladies and gentlemen, it is my pleasure to present you this book on the subject of depression. The book is suitable for every lover of psychology, medicine, pharmacology, as well as for any professional in the field of physical and psychological health care.

The topic of depression has been and will be relevant and important for each of us, as each of us may suffer from similar conditions or disorders.

The book is a wonderful introduction to the specifics of depressive disorders. It can be a useful advisor to each of us in our daily lives, but it can also be a good guide for taking the right steps and measures when we notice that our friend, relative, loved one is suffering.

I hope this book will be useful for

each of you. I also hope it will help you acquire the necessary knowledge, skills and competencies in the fight against depression.

Best regards,
Valentin Boyadzhiev

About the author

Valentin Boyadzhiev is a trained nutritionist, graduated Master of Psychology in "Psychology and Psychopathology of Development". He has acquired Professional Qualification "Teacher of Psychology" and Postgraduate Professional Qualification "Psychological Counseling in Psychosomatic and Social Adaptation Disorders". He has obtained a Psychoanalysis Diploma and he has specialized in Psychoanalytic Psychotherapy. He is a member of the Association "Bulgarian Psychoanalytic Space", "International Society of Applied Psychoanalysis" and „International Alliance of Holistic Therapists". He is a lecturer on issues related to nutrition, diet, supplementation, food, and sports. He is also a teacher and a lecturer in the field of psychology, logic, ethics, law, and philosophy. He has been a school psychologist since 2017. He has been participating annually in scientific conferences on psychology, psychotherapy, dietetics, and medicine. His main interest and practice are in the field of psychoanalysis and clinical psychology.

What is Depression?

According to WHO (World Health Organization) depression is a common illness worldwide, with more than 264 million people affected. Depression is different from usual mood fluctuations and short-lived emotional responses to challenges in everyday life. Especially when long-lasting and with moderate or severe intensity, depression may become a serious health condition. It can cause the affected person to suffer greatly and function poorly at work, at school and in the family. At its worst, depression can lead to suicide. Close to 800 000 people die due to suicide every year. Suicide is the second leading cause of death in 15-29-year-olds. Although there are known, effective treatments for mental disorders, between 76% and 85% of people in low- and middle-income countries receive no treatment for their disorder. Barriers to effective care include a lack of resources, lack of trained health-care providers and social stigma associated with mental disorders. Another barrier to effective care is an inaccurate assessment. In countries of all income levels, people who are depressed are often not correctly diagnosed, and others who do not have the disorder are too often misdiagnosed and prescribed antidepressants. The burden of depression and other mental health conditions is on the rise globally. A World Health Assembly resolution passed in May 2013 has called for a comprehensive, coordinated response to mental disorders at the country level.

According to the National Institute of Mental Health depression is a common but serious mood disorder. It causes severe symptoms that affect how you feel, think, and handle daily activities, such as sleeping, eating, or working. To be diagnosed with depression, the symptoms must be present for at least two weeks.

According to the American Psychiatric Association depression is a common and serious medical illness that negatively affects how you feel, the way you think and how you act. Fortunately, it is also treatable. Depression causes feelings of sadness and/or a loss of interest in activities once enjoyed. It can lead to a variety of emotional and physical problems and can decrease a person's ability to function at work and home. Also, medical conditions (e.g., thyroid problems, a brain tumour or vitamin deficiency) can mimic symptoms of depression so it is important to rule out general medical causes. Depression affects an estimated one in 15 adults (6.7%) in any given year. And one in six people (16.6%) will experience depression at some time in their life. Depression can strike at any time, but on average, first appears during the late teens to mid-20s. Women are more likely than men to experience depression. Some studies show that one-third of women will experience a major depressive episode in their lifetime.

Depression Is Different From Sadness or Grief/Bereavement! The death of a loved one, loss of a job or the ending of a relationship are difficult experiences for a person to endure. It is normal for feelings of sadness or grief to develop in response to such situations. Those experiencing loss often might describe themselves as being "depressed." But being sad is not the same as having depression. The grieving process is natural and unique to each individual and shares some of the same features of depression. Both grief and depression may involve intense sadness and withdrawal from usual activities. They are also different in important ways:

1. In grief, painful feelings come in waves, often intermixed with positive memories of the deceased. In major depression, mood and/or interest (pleasure) are decreased for most of two weeks.

2. In grief, self-esteem is usually maintained. In major depression, feelings of worthlessness and self-loathing are common.

3. For some people, the death of a loved one can bring on major depression. Losing a job or being a victim of a physical assault or a major disaster can lead to depression for some people. When grief and depression co-exist, grief is more

severe and lasts longer than grief without depression. Despite some overlap between grief and depression, they are different. Distinguishing between them can help people get the help, support or treatment they need.

Signs and symptoms of depression:

- a loss of sexual desire;

- agitation, restlessness, irritability, frustration, or restlessness, and pacing up and down;

- slowed movement and speech;

- recurrent thoughts of death or suicide, or an attempt at suicide;

- Appetite and/or weight changes;

- Aches or pains, headaches, cramps, or digestive problems without a clear physical cause and/or that do not ease even with treatment;

- Persistent feelings of sadness, hopelessness, worthlessness, guilt or emptiness;

- Loss of interest in activities or hobbies that used to be enjoyable;

- Difficulty sleeping, sleep disturbances or sleeping too much;

- Difficulty thinking clearly, remembering, concentrating, or making decisions;

- Loss of energy or increased fatigue;

- Increase in purposeless physical activity (e.g., hand-wringing or pacing) or slowed movements and speech (actions observable by others).

In females

Depression is nearly twice as common among women as men, according to the Centers for Disease Control and Prevention (CDC). Below are some symptoms of depression that tend to appear more often in females:

- irritability

- anxiety

- mood swings

- fatigue

- ruminating (in the sense of dwelling on negative thoughts)

Also, some types of depression are unique to females, such as:

- postpartum depression

- premenstrual dysphoric disorder

In males

Around 9% of men in the United States have feelings of depression or anxiety, according to the American Psychological Association. Males with depression are more likely than females to drink alcohol in excess, display anger, and engage in risk-taking as a result of the disorder. Other symptoms of depression in males may include:

- avoiding families and social situations
- working without a break
- having difficulty keeping up with work and family responsibilities
- displaying abusive or controlling behaviour in relationships

In college students

Time at college can be stressful, and a person may be dealing with other lifestyles, cultures, and experiences for the first time. Some students have difficulty coping with these changes, and they may develop depression, anxiety, or both as a result. Symptoms of depression in college students may include:

- difficulty concentrating on schoolwork
- insomnia
- sleeping too much
- a decrease or increase in appetite
- avoiding social situations and activities that they used to enjoy

In teens

Physical changes, peer pressure, and other factors can contribute to depression in teenagers. They may experience some of the following symptoms:

- withdrawing from friends and family
- difficulty concentrating on

schoolwork

- feeling guilty, helpless, or worthless
- restlessness, such as an inability to sit still

In children

The CDC estimate that, in the U.S., 3.2% of children and teens aged 3–17 have a diagnosis of depression. In children, symptoms can make schoolwork and social activities challenging. They may experience symptoms such as:

- crying
- low energy
- clinginess
- defiant behaviour
- vocal outbursts

Younger children may have difficulty expressing how they feel in words. This can make it harder for them to explain their feelings of sadness.

Not everyone who is depressed experiences every symptom. Some people experience only a few symptoms while others may experience many. Several persistent symptoms in addition to low mood are required for a diagnosis of major depression, but people with only a few – but distressing – symptoms may benefit from treatment of their "subsyndromal" depression. The severity and frequency of symptoms and how long they last will vary depending on the individual and his or her particular illness. Symptoms may also vary depending on the stage of the illness.

Risk Factors

According to National Institute of Mental Health depression is one of the most common mental disorders in the U.S. Current research suggests that depression is caused by a combination of genetic, biological, environmental, and psychological factors. Depression can happen at any age but often begins in adulthood. Depression is now recognized as occurring in children and adolescents, although it sometimes presents with more prominent irritability than low mood. Many chronic mood and anxiety disorders in adults begin as high levels of anxiety in children. Depression, especially in midlife or older adults, can co-occur with other serious medical illnesses, such as diabetes, cancer, heart disease, and Parkinson's disease. These conditions are often worse when depression is present. Sometimes medications taken for these physical illnesses may cause side effects that contribute to depression.

Despite what you may have seen in TV ads, read in newspaper articles, or maybe even heard from a doctor, depression is not just the result of a chemical imbalance in the brain, having too much or too little of any brain chemical that can be simply cured with medication. Biological factors can certainly play a role in depression, including inflammation, hormonal changes, immune system suppression, abnormal activity in certain parts of the brain, nutritional deficiencies, and shrinking brain cells. But psychological and social factors—such as past trauma, substance abuse, loneliness, low self-esteem, and lifestyle choices—can also play an enormous part. While some illnesses have a specific medical cause, making treatment straightforward, depression is far more complicated. Certain medications, such as barbiturates, corticosteroids, benzodiazepines, opioid pain killers, and specific blood pressure medicine can trigger depression symptoms in some people—as can hyperthyroidism (an underactive thyroid gland). But most commonly, depression is caused by a combination of biological, psychological, and social factors that can vary wildly from one person to another.

Several factors can play a role in depression:

Biochemistry: Differences in certain chemicals in the brain may contribute to symptoms of depression. Hormone changes (menstrual cycles, pregnancy). Certain medications (sleeping aids, blood pressure medication).

Genetics: Depression can run in families. For example, if one identical twin has depression, the other has a 70 percent chance of having the illness sometime in life. However, there is no single "depression" gene. And just because a close relative suffers from depression, it doesn't mean you will, too. Your lifestyle choices, relationships, and coping skills matter just as much as genetics.

Personality: Whether your personality traits are inherited from your parents or the result of life experiences, they can impact your risk of depression. For example, you may be at greater risk if you tend to worry excessively, have a negative outlook on life, are highly self-critical. People with low self-esteem, who are easily overwhelmed by stress, or who are generally pessimistic appear to be more likely to experience depression.

Environmental factors: There's a strong relationship between **loneliness** and depression. Not only can lack social support heighten your risk for depression but having depression can cause you to withdraw from others, exacerbating feelings of isolation. Having close friends or family to talk to can help you maintain perspective on your issues and avoid having to deal with problems alone. While a network of strong and supportive relationships can be crucial to good mental health, **troubled, unhappy, or abusive relationships** can have the opposite effect and increase your risk for depression. **Major life changes**, such as a bereavement, divorce, unemployment, or financial problems can often bring overwhelming levels of stress and increase your risk of developing depression. **Early life stresses** such as childhood trauma, abuse, or bullying can make you more susceptible to some future health conditions, including depression. **Substance abuse** can often co-occur with depression. Many people use alcohol or drugs as a means of self-medicating their moods or cope with stress or difficult emotions. If you are already at risk for depression, abusing alcohol or drugs may push you over the edge. There is also evidence that those who abuse opioid painkillers are at greater risk for depression. **Unmanaged pain** or being diagnosed with a serious illness, such as cancer, heart disease, or diabetes, can trigger feelings of hopelessness and even lead to depression. The stress and worry of coping with a **serious illness** can lead to depression, especially if you're dealing with long-term management and/or chronic pain.

Depression most often results from a combination of factors, rather than one single cause. For example, if you went through a divorce, were diagnosed with a serious medical condition, or lost your job, the stress could prompt you to start drinking more, which in turn could cause you to withdraw from family and friends. Those factors combined could then trigger depression. It's important to remember that you can't always identify the cause of depression or change difficult circumstances. The most important thing is to recognise the signs and symptoms and seek support.

Forms of Depression

There are different forms of depression:

Major depression is sometimes called a major depressive disorder, clinical depression, unipolar depression or simply 'depression'. It involves low mood and/or loss of interest and pleasure in usual activities, as well as other symptoms. The symptoms are experienced most days and last for at least two weeks and interfere with your ability to work, sleep, study, eat, and enjoy life. Symptoms of depression interfere with all areas of a person's life. Major depression, as we discussed, is the most common type of depression. Often, people with major depression experience recurrent episodes throughout their lives.

Persistent depressive disorder (dysthymia) is a depressed mood that lasts for at least two years. It could be described as feeling like you're living on autopilot. A person diagnosed with persistent depressive disorder may have episodes of major depression along with periods of less severe symptoms, but symptoms must last for two years to be considered a persistent depressive disorder. The symptoms of dysthymia are similar to those of major depression but are less severe. However, in the case of dysthymia, symptoms last longer.

Perinatal Depression or postpartum depression: Women with perinatal depression experience full-blown major depression during pregnancy or after delivery (postpartum depression). Postpartum depression is much more serious than the "baby blues" (relatively mild depressive and anxiety symptoms that typically clear within two weeks after delivery) that many women experience after giving birth. Women with postpartum depression experience full-blown major depression during pregnancy or after delivery (postpartum depression). The feelings of extreme sadness, anxiety, and exhaustion that accompany postpartum depression may make it difficult for these new mothers to complete daily care activities for themselves and/or for their babies. Women are at an increased risk of depression during pregnancy (known as the antenatal or prenatal period) and in the year following childbirth (known as the postnatal period). You may also come across the term 'perinatal', which describes the period covered by pregnancy and the first year after the baby's birth. The causes of depression at this time can be complex and are often the result of a combination of factors. In the days immediately following birth, many women experience the 'baby blues' which is a common condition related to hormonal changes and affects up to 80 percent of women. The 'baby blues', or general stress adjusting to pregnancy and/or a new baby, are common experiences but are different from depression. Depression is longer lasting and can affect not only the mother but her relationship with her baby, the child's development, the mother's relationship with her partner and with other members of the family. Almost 10 percent of women will experience depression during pregnancy. This increases to 16 percent in the first three months after having a baby.

Seasonal Affective Disorder is a type of depression that comes and goes with the seasons, typically starting in the late fall and early winter and going away during the spring and summer. Winter depression, typically accompanied by social withdrawal, increased sleep, and weight gain, predictably returns every year in seasonal affective disorder. The cause of the disorder is unclear, but it's thought to be related to the variation in light exposure in different seasons. It's characterised by mood disturbances (either periods of depression or mania) that begin and end in a particular season. It's usually diagnosed after the person has had the same symptoms during winter for a couple of years. People with SAD (Seasonal Affective Disorder) depression are more likely to experience a lack of energy, sleep too much, overeat, gain weight and crave for carbohydrates.

Psychotic Depression: This type of depression occurs when a person has severe depression plus some form of psychosis, such as having disturbing false fixed beliefs (delusions) or hearing or seeing upsetting things that others cannot hear or see (hallucinations). The psychotic symptoms typically have a depressive "theme," such as delusions of guilt, poverty, or illness. They can also be paranoid, feeling as though everyone is against them.

Bipolar disorder is also called Manic Depressive Disorder because it involves alternating between mania and depressive episodes. It is different from depression, but it is included in this list because someone with bipolar disorder could experience episodes of extremely low moods that meet the criteria for major depression. But a person with bipolar disorder also experiences extreme high – euphoric or irritable – moods called "mania" or a less severe form called "hypomania." Mania is like the opposite of depression and can vary in intensity – symptoms include feeling great, having lots of energy, having racing thoughts and little need for sleep, talking quickly, having difficulty focusing on tasks, and feeling frustrated and irritable. This is not just a fleeting experience. Sometimes the person loses touch with reality and has episodes of psychosis. Experiencing psychosis involves hallucinations (seeing or hearing something that is not there) or having delusions (e.g. the person believing he or she has superpowers). Bipolar disorder seems to be most closely linked to family history. Stress and conflict can trigger episodes for people with this condition and it's not uncommon for bipolar disorder to be misdiagnosed as depression, alcohol or drug abuse, attention deficit hyperactivity disorder (ADHD) or schizophrenia. Diagnosis depends on the person having an episode of mania and unless observed, this can be hard to detect. It is not uncommon for people to go for years before receiving an accurate diagnosis of bipolar disorder. If you're experiencing highs and lows, it's helpful to make this clear to your doctor or treating health professional. Bipolar disorder affects approximately 2 percent of the population.

Cyclothymic disorder: Cyclothymic disorder is often described as a milder form of bipolar disorder. The person experiences chronic fluctuating moods over at least two years, involving periods of hypomania (a mild to moderate level of mania) and periods of depressive symptoms, with very short periods (no more than two months) of normality between. The duration of the symptoms are shorter, less severe and not as regular, and therefore don't fit the criteria of bipolar disorder or major depression.

Melancholia: This is the term used to describe a severe form of depression where many of the physical symptoms of depression are present. One of the major changes is that the person starts to move more slowly. They're also more likely to have a depressed mood that is characterised by complete loss of pleasure in everything, or almost everything.

Situational Depression is triggered by a life-changing event. It could be anything, from losing your job to the death of a close family member.

Premenstrual Dysphoric Disorder is severe depression that shows up a week or two before the period starts. It affects the individual's ability to function normally.

Atypical Depression refers to a depressive state where individuals experience improved mood when encountering pleasurable events. This type of major depression, or dysthymia, is atypical of melancholic depression, where mood improvements from positive situations do not typically manifest in affected individuals.

Major Depression

Major depression, also known as unipolar or major depressive disorder, is characterized by a persistent feeling of sadness or a lack of interest in outside stimuli. Unipolar depression is solely focused on the "lows," or the negative emotions and symptoms that you may have experienced. Fortunately, major depression is well understood in the medical community and is often easily treatable through a combination of medication and talk therapy.

Signs and Symptoms:

- Fatigue or loss of energy almost every day;
- Feelings of worthlessness or guilt almost every day;
- Impaired concentration,

indecisiveness;
- Insomnia or hypersomnia (excessive sleeping) almost every day;
- Markedly diminished interest or pleasure in almost all activities nearly every day (called anhedonia, this symptom can be indicated by reports from significant others);
- Restlessness or feeling slowed down;
- Recurring thoughts of death or suicide;
- Significant weight loss or gain (a change of more than 5% of body weight in a month);

Causes: It's not known exactly what causes depression. As with many mental disorders, a variety of factors may be involved, such as:

- **Biological differences.** People with

depression appear to have physical changes in their brains. The significance of these changes is still uncertain, but may eventually help pinpoint causes.

- **Brain chemistry.** Neurotransmitters are naturally occurring brain chemicals that likely play a role in depression. Recent research indicates that changes in the function and effect of these neurotransmitters and how they interact with neurocircuits involved in maintaining mood stability may play a significant role in depression and its treatment.

- **Hormones.** Changes in the body's balance of hormones may be involved in causing or triggering depression. Hormone changes can be a result of pregnancy and during the weeks or months after delivery (postpartum) and from thyroid problems, menopause or a number of other conditions.

- **Inherited traits.** Depression is more common in people whose blood relatives also have this condition. Researchers are trying to find genes that may be involved in causing depression.

Treatment: The most helpful treatment is a combination of psychotherapy and **medication**. Selective serotonin reuptake inhibitors (SSRIs) are commonly prescribed first. SSRIs are known to cause problems with sexual functioning, some nausea, and an increase in anxiety in the early stages of treatment. Older classes of antidepressants, tricyclic antidepressants and monoamine oxidase inhibitors are still in use. They are as effective as the newer ones and can be very useful when someone has not responded well to other treatments.

It usually takes at least two to six weeks of taking an antidepressant to see improvement. It may take several trials to find the medication that works best. Once the right medication is found, it may take up to a few months to find a proper dose and for the full positive effect to be seen. Sometimes, two different antidepressants are used together.

Psychotherapy, also known as psychological therapy or talk therapy, can be an effective treatment for people with MDD. It involves meeting with a therapist regularly to talk about your condition and related issues. Psychotherapy can help you:

- adjust to a crisis or other stressful event;
- replace negative beliefs and behaviours with positive, healthy ones;
- improve your communication skills;

- find better ways to cope with challenges and solve problems;
- increase your self-esteem;
- regain a sense of satisfaction and control in your life.

Your healthcare provider may also recommend other types of therapy, such as cognitive-behavioural therapy or interpersonal therapy. Another possible treatment is group therapy, which allows you to share your feelings with people who can relate to what you're going through.

In some situations, a treatment called **electroconvulsive therapy (ECT)** can be a life-saving option. This treatment is controversial but very effective. In ECT, an electrical impulse is applied to the person's scalp and passes to the brain, causing a seizure. The patient is under anaesthesia and is monitored carefully. Medication is given before the procedure to prevent any outward signs of convulsions, which helps to prevent injury. Improvement is seen gradually over a period of days to weeks after the treatment. ECT is the quickest and most effective treatment for the most severe forms of depression, and in most people, it is not riskier than other antidepressant treatments.

Persistent depressive disorder (dysthymia)

Persistent depressive disorder (dysthymia) is a form of depression. It may be less severe than major depression, but — as the name suggests — it lasts longer. People with dysthymia describe their mood as sad or "down in the dumps," but dysthymia is more than simply feeling sad. Dysthymia is a chronic form of depression that can cause people to lose interest in normal daily activities, have low self-esteem and an overall feeling of inadequacy, feelings of hopelessness, and difficulty with productivity. Given the chronic nature of dysthymia, these feelings can last for years and negatively impact relationships, employment, education, and other daily activities. People with dysthymia often find it difficult to be "upbeat", even during good times. They might be perceived as gloomy, pessimistic, or a complainer.

Causes of dysthymia: The exact cause of dysthymia is unknown, but as with major depressive disorder it may include more than one cause, including some of the following:

- **Brain chemistry** – some brain regions have been implicated in dysthymia;
- **Genetics** – having a first degree relative with a depressive disorder increases the risk;
- **Environmental/life events** – loss of a parent during childhood, traumatic events such as loss, financial problems, and high levels of stress can trigger dysthymia;
- **Personality traits** that include negativity – low self-esteem,

pessimistic, self-critical, dependent upon others;
- **History** of other mental disorders.

Symptoms of dysthymia: The essential feature of dysthymia is a depressed mood that occurs for most of the day, for more days than not, for at least two years for adults or one year for children and adolescents. Symptoms of dysthymia can come and go over time, and the intensity of the symptoms can change, but symptoms generally don't disappear for more than two months at a time. Symptoms of dysthymia can include:

- Poor appetite or overeating
- Loss of interest in daily activities
- Insomnia or hypersomnia
- Low energy or fatigue
- Low self-esteem, self-criticism, or feeling incapable

- Poor concentration or difficulty making decisions
- Feelings of hopelessness
- Decreased activity and/or productivity
- Social isolation
- Irritability or anger
- Sadness or feeling down
- Feelings of guilt
- In children, depressed mood and irritability are often primary symptoms.

Treatment: Treatments for persistent depressive disorder include medications and psychotherapy, including cognitive-behavioural therapy and interpersonal therapy. Medications are believed to be a more effective treatment than psychotherapy when used alone, but a combination of medication and psychotherapy is believed to be the most effective treatment. Medications include selective serotonin reuptake inhibitors (SSRIs), serotonin and norepinephrine reuptake inhibitors (SNRIs) and tricyclic antidepressants (TCAs). Children and young adults should be closely monitored by their health-care providers and their families when taking antidepressants, especially when they have just begun taking them or when their dose has recently been changed. It's important to ask your doctor for detailed information about any potential side effects of medication and to discuss any history of suicidal thoughts or attempts. Though antidepressant medications can cause uncomfortable side effects for some, you should never abruptly stop taking these medications. Always consult your prescribing physician before making any changes to medication.

Psychotherapy: Talk therapy, or counselling, is a general form of treating dysthymia by discussing your symptoms and how they impact your life with a mental health provider. There are many benefits to psychotherapy, including:

Crisis and symptom management
Identifying triggers that contribute to your dysthymia and coping strategies to manage them;
Identifying negative beliefs and replacing them with positive ones;
Learning adaptive problem-solving skills;
Exploring ways to build positive relationships with others;
Improving self-esteem;
Learning to set and attain personal goals.

There are different kinds of psychotherapy available, and many people require a combination of treatments. Talk to your mental health provider about the options.

Seasonal affective disorder

Seasonal affective disorder (SAD) is a category of depression that emerges in particular seasons of the year. Most people notice SAD symptoms starting in the fall and increasing during the winter months, but a few people experience a spring/summer version. Let's take a look at some common questions you might have about this disorder.

SAD symptoms: In most cases, seasonal affective disorder symptoms appear during late fall or early winter and go away during the sunnier days of spring and summer. Less commonly, people with the opposite pattern have symptoms that begin in spring or summer. In either case, symptoms may start out mild and become more severe as the season progresses. Signs and symptoms of SAD may include:

- Feeling depressed most of the day, nearly every day;
- Losing interest in activities you once enjoyed;
- Having low energy;
- Having problems with sleeping;
- Experiencing changes in your appetite or weight;
- Feeling sluggish or agitated;
- Having difficulty concentrating;
- Feeling hopeless, worthless or guilty;
- Having frequent thoughts of death or suicide.

Causes: The specific cause of the seasonal affective disorder remains unknown. Some factors that may come into play include:

- **Your biological clock** (circadian rhythm). The reduced level of sunlight in fall and winter may cause winter-onset SAD. This decrease in sunlight may disrupt your body's internal clock and lead to feelings of depression.
- **Serotonin levels.** A drop in serotonin, a brain chemical (neurotransmitter) that affects mood, might play a role in SAD. Reduced sunlight can cause a drop in serotonin that may trigger depression.
- **Melatonin levels.** The change in season can disrupt the balance of the body's level of melatonin, which plays a role in sleep patterns and mood.

Treatment: SAD can be effectively treated in several ways, including light therapy, antidepressant medications, talk therapy or some combination of these. While symptoms will generally improve on their own with the change of season, symptoms can improve more quickly with treatment.

Medication – Antidepressants have proven to be effective for people with SAD, especially those with intense symptoms. Medication requires patience because it can take several weeks before you begin to feel the effects. It's also important not to stop taking the medication if you feel better. Consult with your doctor before you change your dosage, and let him or her know if you experience any side effects.

Psychotherapy – Talk therapy can be an invaluable option for those with SAD. A psychotherapist can help you identify patterns in negative thinking and behaviour that impact depression, learn positive ways of coping with symptoms, and institute relaxation techniques that can help you restore lost energy.

Light therapy – Phototherapy involves exposing oneself to light via a special box or lamp. This device produces similar effects to natural light, triggering chemicals in your brain that help regulate your mood. This treatment has proven effective especially for those who experience the winter version of SAD. Don't make an impulse buy on the Internet though, as it's important to consult with your doctor first. You want to make sure you've purchased an effective and safe device.

Psychotic depression

Psychotic depression, also known as a major depressive disorder with psychotic features, is a serious condition that requires immediate treatment and close monitoring by a medical or mental health professional. Major depressive disorder with mood-congruent psychotic features means that the content of the hallucinations and delusions is consistent with typical depressive themes. These may include feelings of personal inadequacy, guilt, or worthlessness. Major depressive disorder with mood-incongruent psychotic features means that the content of the hallucinations and delusions don't involve typical depressive themes. Some people may also experience a combination of both mood-congruent and mood-incongruent themes in their delusions and hallucinations. It's estimated that anywhere from 14 to nearly 50% of people diagnosed with depression have psychotic depression, and geriatric patients are especially prone to it. Psychotic depression is taken very seriously by mental health professionals because the individual suffering from it is at an increased risk of self-harm.

Symptoms: To be called a psychotic depression, according to the fifth edition of the *Diagnostic and Statistical Manual of Mental Disorders*, major depression must be present along with delusions and/or hallucinations. If psychotic features are present, they must be either mood-congruent (having to do with typical depressive themes like personal inadequacy, death, or deserved punishment) or non-mood-congruent (in other words, not involving the depressive themes). Typically, the psychotic symptoms have a depressive "theme," such as delusions of guilt, poverty, or illness. Typically, the person with psychotic depression exhibits a low, sad mood, with poor concentration and feelings of lack of self-worth and guilt. One of the reasons that psychotic depression is not easily diagnosed, he says, is that people with psychotic depression often realize that their thoughts may not be "quite right" so they keep them to themselves.

People with psychotic depression have symptoms of major depression along with psychosis. The symptoms of major depression include:

- fatigue;
- irritability;
- difficulty concentrating;
- feelings of hopelessness or helplessness;
- feelings of worthlessness or self-

hate;

- social isolation;
- loss of interest in activities once found pleasurable;
- sleeping too little or too much;
- changes in appetite;
- sudden weight loss or weight gain;
- talks or threats of suicide.

In addition to the above symptoms, people with psychotic depression will also experience **delusions** (thoughts or beliefs that are unlikely to be true) and/or **hallucinations** (hearing and, in some cases, feeling, smelling, seeing or tasting things that are not there; hearing voices is a common hallucination).

Risk Factors: One of the biggest risk factors is childhood trauma, says Dr. Rothschild. "Early life trauma puts you at risk," he says. "The loss of a parent before age 11, for instance, or any trauma such as sexual or physical abuse puts you at risk. And if a person with these risk factors gets depressed as an adult, they are at a higher risk for psychotic depression." Additionally, it's more likely for people to develop psychotic depression as they get older. "Psychotic depression can occur in any age group but it is not uncommon for someone with no prior psychiatric history to present with psychotic depression in their 60s, 70s, or 80s," Dr. Rothschild says. "In older people, delusions of poverty or somatic delusions, for example, believing one is suffering from a fatal illness, are more likely to be present."

Treatment: There is some debate around the best treatment process for psychotic depression, particularly regarding first- and second-line treatments. First-line treatment usually involves a combination of antidepressant and antipsychotic medications, or monotherapy, which refers to the use of either antidepressants or antipsychotics alone. Common choices include serotonin reuptake inhibitors (SSRIs) or serotonin-norepinephrine reuptake inhibitors (SNRIs). Research has found that the combination of antidepressant and antipsychotic drugs is more effective than using either medication on its own. Doctors typically reserve electroconvulsive therapy (ECT) for second-line treatment, and specialists may use it if different medications have not helped to alleviate symptoms. Electroconvulsive therapy (ECT) is a medical procedure performed under anaesthesia, in which a doctor, usually a psychiatrist, applies electrical currents to a person's head, inducing a generalized seizure in the brain. The treating prescriber may refer a person to electroconvulsive therapy (ECT) if they do not respond to medication-based treatments. Electroconvulsive therapy is a safe and effective treatment for people with psychotic depression. Psychotherapy, or talking therapies, can also help people, as a supplemental treatment for depression with psychosis.

Bipolar Disorder. Manic Depression. Bipolar Affective Disorder

Bipolar Disorder, Manic Depression, Bipolar Affective Disorder. All three terms are synonymous with each other and the name of a mental health disorder. The classic symptoms of bipolar disorder are the periodic changes in mood, alternating between periods of elevated mood (mania or hypomania) and periods of depression. If you are living with bipolar disorder, you may feel energetic, abnormally happy, and make reckless or impulsive decisions during manic states. During depressive states, you may feel the overwhelming urge to cry, experience feelings of hopelessness, and have a negative outlook on life. Hypomania is a less severe form of mania, where you generally feel pretty good–with a better sense of well-being and productivity. With bipolar disorder, you don't just feel "down in the dumps;" your depressive state may lead to suicidal thoughts that change over to feelings of euphoria and endless energy. These extreme mood swings can occur more frequently — such as every week. Or, show up more sporadically — maybe just twice a year. There is also no defined pattern to the mood swings. One does not always occur before the other — and the length of time you are in one state or the other varies as well. Rates of bipolar disorder in men and women are about equal and the typical onset of symptoms occur around 25 years of age.

Types of bipolar disorder: There are three main types of bipolar disorder: bipolar I, bipolar II, and cyclothymia.

- **Bipolar I** is defined by the appearance of at least one manic episode. You may experience hypomanic or major depressive episodes before and after the manic episode. This type of bipolar disorder affects men and women equally.

- People with **bipolar II** disorder experience one major depressive episode that lasts at least two weeks. They also have at least one hypomanic episode that lasts about four days. This type of bipolar disorder is thought to be more common in women.

- People with **cyclothymia** have episodes of hypomania and depression. These symptoms are shorter and less severe than the mania and depression caused by bipolar I or bipolar II disorder. Most people with this condition only experience a month or two at a time where their moods are stable.

Signs and Symptoms of Bipolar Disorder: Because there are many different stages of bipolar disorder, the signs and symptoms vary from person to person and from type to type. Presented below are the most common signs and symptoms of bipolar disorder, categorized by emotional state.

Manic Symptoms: According to the DSM-5, a manic episode is characterized by a distinct and abnormal state of elevated, expansive, or irritable mood occurring for at least one week. The manic episode is persistently driven by goal-directed behaviour or energy. A hypomanic episode is a distinct and abnormal state of elevated, expansive, or irritable mood that lasts for at least four consecutive days. If you have been diagnosed as suffering from bipolar disorder, you may experience any of the signs and symptoms during a manic period:

- A long period of feeling "high" — an overly elated, happy, and outgoing mood;
- Feeling extremely irritable;
- Being easily distracted;
- Having racing thoughts;
- Talking very fast;
- Jumping from one thought to another when talking;
- Taking on a lot of new projects;
- Restlessness;
- Boundless energy;
- Sleeping very little;
- Not feeling tired;
- Unrealistically believing you can do

something;

- Engaging in impulsive, pleasurable, and high-risk behaviours (i.e. poor financial investments, sexual indiscretions, shopping sprees);
- Inflated self-esteem;
- Feelings of grandiosity;
- Increased agitation;
- Increased goal-directed activity;
- High sex drive;
- Making grand and unattainable plans;
- Detachment from reality — psychosis that may include delusions or hallucinations.

Manic behaviours interfere with functioning at school or work, in social situations, and in relationships. These behaviours occur on their own — they do not occur due to alcohol or drug use, a medical illness, or a side effect of a medication.

Depressive Symptoms: The depressive side of bipolar disorder is characterized by a major depressive episode resulting in a depressed mood or loss of interest or pleasure in life. If you are living with bipolar disorder, during depressive states, you may experience some of the following signs and symptoms:

- Feeling sad, tearful, hopeless, or empty for the majority of the day on a daily basis;
- No pleasure or interest in day to day activities;
- Weight fluctuations — including significant weight loss or weight gain;
- Sleep disturbances — sleeping too much or other sleep problems, such

as insomnia;

- Restlessness or slowed behaviours;
- Suicidal thoughts, planning, or attempts;
- Feelings of guilt and worthlessness;
- Inability to concentrate;
- Indecisiveness;
- Loss of energy;
- Feelings of fatigue;
- Psychosis — being detached from reality; delusions or hallucinations;
- Loss of interest in activities you once enjoyed;
- Anxiety;
- Uncontrollable crying.

Depressive behaviours can interfere with school or work, family or personal relationships, and social functioning. If you are suffering from bipolar disorder and undergoing a depressive episode, it is not the result of substance abuse, medications, an underlying medical condition, or stressful situation – such as grieving the loss of a loved one.

Causes: Scientists have not yet discovered a single cause of the disorder. Currently, they believe several factors may contribute, including:

- **Genetics**. The chances of developing bipolar disorder are increased if a child's parents or siblings have the disorder. But the role of genetics is not absolute: A child from a family with a history of bipolar disorder may never develop the disorder. Studies of identical twins have found that, even if one twin develops the disorder, the other may not.
- **Stress**. A stressful event such as a death in the family, an illness, a

difficult relationship, divorce or financial problems can trigger a manic or depressive episode. Thus, a person's handling of stress may also play a role in the development of the illness.

- **Brain structure and function.** Brain scans cannot diagnose bipolar disorder, yet researchers have identified subtle differences in the average size or activation of some brain structures in people with bipolar disorder.

Diagnosis: If your GP thinks you may have bipolar disorder, they'll usually refer you to a psychiatrist, a doctor who specialises in mental health problems. You'll be assessed by the psychiatrist at your appointment. They'll ask you a few questions to find out if you have bipolar disorder. If you do, they'll decide what treatments are most suitable. During the assessment, you'll be asked about your symptoms and when you first experienced them. The psychiatrist will also ask about how you feel leading up to and during an episode of mania or depression, and if you have thoughts about harming yourself. The psychiatrist will also want to know about your medical background and family history, especially whether any of your relatives have had bipolar disorder. If someone else in your family has the condition, the psychiatrist may want to talk to them. But they'll ask for your agreement before doing so. To be diagnosed with bipolar disorder, a person must have experienced at least one episode of mania or hypomania. Mental health care professionals use the Diagnostic and Statistical Manual of Mental Disorders (DSM) to diagnose the "type" of bipolar disorder a person may be experiencing. To determine what type of bipolar disorder a person has, mental health care professionals assess the pattern of symptoms and how impaired the person is during their most severe episodes.

Treatment: Medications and psychotherapy are the most commonly prescribed treatment plans for people suffering from bipolar disorder. And the success rate of these treatment plans is great if followed correctly and consistently.

Medication: Certain medications can help manage symptoms of bipolar disorder. Medications generally used to treat bipolar disorder include mood stabilizers and second-generation ("atypical") antipsychotics. Treatment plans may also include medications that target sleep or anxiety. Health care providers often prescribe antidepressant medication to treat depressive episodes in bipolar disorder, combining the antidepressant with a mood stabilizer to prevent triggering a manic episode.

According to National Institute of Mental Health **"Psychotherapy**, also called "talk therapy," can be an effective part of the treatment plan for people with bipolar disorder. Psychotherapy is a term for a variety of treatment techniques that aim to help a person identify and change troubling emotions, thoughts, and behaviours. It can provide support, education, and guidance to people with bipolar disorder and their families. Treatment may include therapies such as cognitive-behavioural therapy (CBT) and psychoeducation, which are used to treat a variety of conditions. Treatment may also include newer therapies designed specifically for the treatment of a bipolar disorder, including interpersonal and social rhythm therapy

(IPSRT) and family-focused therapy. Determining whether intensive psychotherapeutic intervention at the earliest stages of bipolar disorder can prevent or limit its full-blown onset is an important area of ongoing research."

Moreover, according to NIMH other types of supporting therapy are used too: "**Electroconvulsive Therapy** (ECT): ECT is a brain stimulation procedure that can help people get relief from severe symptoms of bipolar disorder. With modern ECT, a person usually goes through a series of treatment sessions over several weeks. ECT is delivered under general anaesthesia and is safe. It can be effective in treating severe depressive and manic episodes, which occur most often when medication and psychotherapy are not effective or are not safe for a particular patient. ECT can also be effective when a rapid response is needed, as in the case of suicide risk or catatonia (a state of unresponsiveness)." and "Transcranial magnetic stimulation (TMS): TMS is a newer approach to brain stimulation that uses magnetic waves. It is delivered to an awake patient most days for 1 month. Research shows that TMS is helpful for many people with various subtypes of depression, but its role in the treatment of the bipolar disorder is still under study."

Atypical depression

Atypical depression is a subtype of major depression or dysthymic disorder that involves several specific symptoms, including increased appetite or weight gain, sleepiness or excessive sleep, marked fatigue or weakness, moods that are strongly reactive to environmental circumstances, and feeling extremely sensitive to rejection. It is a depressive state where individuals experience improved mood when encountering pleasurable events. An increased risk of suicide and anxiety disorders is present with atypical depression. Some researchers believe that atypical depression is due to key brain differences, inclusive of abnormal chemical neurotransmitters carrying signals to the brain and body, and heredity.

Symptoms of atypical depression can vary from person to person. Key signs and symptoms may include:

- Depression that temporarily lifts in response to good news or positive events;
- Increased appetite or weight gain;
- Sleeping too much but still feeling sleepy in the daytime;
- Heavy, leaden feeling in your arms or legs that lasts an hour or more in a day;
- Sensitivity to rejection or criticism, which affects your relationships, social life or job;
- For some people, signs and symptoms of atypical depression can be severe, such as feeling suicidal or not being able to do basic day-to-day activities.

Causes: It's not known exactly what causes atypical depression or why some people have different features of depression. Atypical depression often starts in the teenage years, earlier than other types of depression, and can have a more long-term (chronic) course. As with other types of depression, a combination of factors may be involved. These include:

- **Brain differences.**Neurotransmitters are naturally occurring brain chemicals that carry signals to other parts of your brain and body. When these chemicals are abnormal or impaired, the function of nerve receptors and nerve systems change, leading to depression.
- **Inherited traits.** Depression is more common in people whose blood relatives also have the condition.

Treatment for MDD with atypical features can vary. In most cases, however, treatment includes a combination of medications, talk therapy, and lifestyle changes. Your doctor may prescribe antidepressants, such as monoamine oxidase inhibitors (MAOIs) or selective serotonin reuptake inhibitors (SSRIs). Some people who have MDD with atypical features don't respond well to tricyclic antidepressants. However, numerous MAOIs and SSRIs have proven effective in treating symptoms of the disorder. Your doctor may prescribe one medication or a combination of medications to control your symptoms. Psychotherapy, which involves dialogue with a mental health professional about your condition and related issues, has also been found to be highly effective in treating atypical depression. During psychotherapy, or talk therapy, sessions, individuals can learn ways to cope, including:

- Identifying and changing unhealthy thoughts or behaviours;
- Discussing relationships and experiences;
- Exploring different coping and problem-solving processes;
- Setting realistic goals;
- Finding ways to ease depressive symptoms.

Postpartum depression

Postpartum depression (PPD) is a complex mix of physical, emotional, and behavioural changes that happen in a woman after giving birth. According to the DSM-5, a manual used to diagnose mental disorders, PPD is a form of major depression that has its onset within four weeks after delivery. The diagnosis of postpartum depression is based not only on the length of time between delivery and onset but also on the severity of the depression. Postpartum depression is a serious mental illness that involves the brain and affects your behaviour and physical health. If you have depression, then sad, flat, or empty feelings don't go away and can interfere with your day-to-day life. You might feel unconnected to your baby, as if you are not the baby's mother, or you might not love or care for the baby. These feelings can be mild to severe. "Postpartum" means the time after childbirth. Most women get the "baby blues," or feel sad or empty, within a few days of giving birth. For many women, the baby blues go away in 3 to 5 days. If your baby blues don't go away or you feel sad, hopeless, or empty for longer than 2 weeks, you may have postpartum depression. Feeling hopeless or empty after childbirth is not a regular or expected part of being a mother.

Symptoms: According to the Centers for Disease Control and Prevention (CDC), up to 20 percent of new mothers experience one or more symptoms of postpartum depression. Similar to other types of depression, PPD can include some symptoms:

- Feeling down or depressed for most of the day for several weeks or more;
- Feeling distant and withdrawn from family and friends;
- A loss of interest in activities (including sex);
- Changes in eating and sleeping habits;
- Feeling tired most of the day;
- Feeling angry or irritable;
- Having feelings of anxiety, worry, panic attacks or racing thoughts.

Postpartum psychosis is a related mental health condition that can also develop after childbirth. This rare and serious condition includes symptoms of hallucinations (seeing or hearing things that aren't there), paranoia, and, at times, thoughts of harming one's self or others. Some mothers have frequent thoughts about harming their children. If you are experiencing signs of postpartum depression or postpartum psychosis, please tell someone. These conditions can be effectively treated and often respond best when treatment is started right away.

Causes: A number of factors can lead to postpartum depression. Women with a history of depression and other mental health conditions face a higher risk of PPD. The following factors can also increase one's risk:

- Hormonal changes that follow childbirth;
- Emotional stressors, including financial strain, job changes, illness, or the death of a loved one;
- Changes in social relationships, or lack of a strong support network;
- Raising a child with special needs or

an infant that is challenging to care for;

- Having a family history of mental health issues.

The following factors may contribute to PPD:

- the physical changes of pregnancy;
- excessive worry about the baby and the responsibilities of being a parent;
- complicated or difficult labour and childbirth;
- lack of family support;
- worries about relationships;
- financial difficulties;
- loneliness, not having close friends and family around;
- a history of mental health problems;
- the health consequences of childbirth, including urinary

incontinence, anemia, blood pressure changes, and alterations in metabolism;

- hormonal changes, due to a sudden and severe drop in estrogen and progesterone levels following birth;
- changes to the sleep cycle.

Treatment:

Therapy. During therapy, you talk to a therapist, psychologist, or social worker to learn strategies to change how depression makes you think, feel, and act. CBT is a type of psychotherapy that can help people with depression and anxiety. It teaches people different ways of thinking, behaving, and reacting to situations. People learn to challenge and change unhelpful patterns of thinking and behaviour as a way of improving their depressive and anxious feelings and emotions. CBT can be conducted individually or with a group of people who have similar concerns. PT is an evidence-based therapy that has been used to treat depression, including perinatal depression. It is based on the idea that interpersonal and life events impact mood and vice versa. The goal of IPT is to help people to improve their communication skills within relationships, to develop social support networks, and to develop realistic expectations that allow them to deal with crises or other issues that may be contributing to their depression.

Medicine. There are different types of medicines for postpartum depression. All of them must be prescribed by your doctor or nurse. The most common type is antidepressants. Antidepressants can help relieve symptoms of depression and some can be taken while you're breastfeeding. Antidepressants may take several weeks to start working.

Electroconvulsive therapy (ECT). This can be used in extreme cases to treat postpartum depression. If the symptoms are so severe that they do not respond to other treatment, they might benefit from electroconvulsive therapy (ECT). However, this only suggested when all other options, such as medication have not been successful. ECT is applied under general anaesthetic and with muscle relaxants. ECT is usually very effective in cases of very severe depression. The benefits, however, may be short-lived. Side effects include headaches and memory loss that is usually, but not always, short term.

Other ways to help yourself: Also, many hospitals offer support groups for new mothers. Staffed by women's health experts, this is a great place to share your feelings in a safe, supportive place with other women who understand what you are going through. Ask your doctor about new mother support groups in your town. The adjustment to motherhood can be very stressful as you learn to navigate your new role, balancing care for yourself and an infant (and possibly other children and family members). This can be demanding, exhausting and overwhelming. If you are a new mom with feelings of anxiety or depression, you may even feel guilty or ashamed. It is important to know that postpartum depression is not your fault. Postpartum depression is a medical condition that can be treated. By sharing your feelings with a professional, you will be on your way to making positive changes that will have a big impact on your daily well-being.

Premenstrual dysphoric disorder

Premenstrual dysphoric disorder (PMDD) is a condition in which a woman has severe depression symptoms, irritability, and tension before menstruation. The symptoms of PMDD are more severe than those seen with premenstrual syndrome (PMS). PMS refers to a wide range of physical or emotional symptoms that most often occur about 5 to 11 days before a woman starts her monthly menstrual cycle. In most cases, the symptoms stop when, or shortly after, her period begins. While up to 85% of women experience PMS, only around 5% of women are diagnosed with PMDD, according to a study in the American Journal of Psychiatry. PMDD can arise at any time during a woman's reproductive years although the average age of onset is 26 years. The symptoms of PMDD begin in the late luteal phase of the menstrual cycle (after ovulation) and end shortly after menstruation begins. While most women have PMS from time to time in the days leading up to their period, the symptoms do not cause any clinically significant distress or impact their ability to continue with their daily activities. However, for women with PMDD, the more severe PMS-related problems—particularly those that are psychological—prevent them from going about their everyday lives. These symptoms do not necessarily occur every cycle, but they are present in the majority of the cycles. Some months may be worse than others. The onset of PMDD may begin at any time after a woman's first period, although many individuals report a worsening of symptoms as they approach menopause. After menopause and during pregnancy, symptoms do not occur, though it is important to note that women with PMDD have a high risk of experiencing postpartum depression following the birth of a child.

To receive a diagnosis of PMDD, a woman must have experienced symptoms during most of the menstrual cycles of the past year and these symptoms must have had an adverse effect on work or social functioning. While the core symptoms relate to mood and anxiety, behavioural and physical symptoms commonly occur also. It is crucial to note that the presence of behavioural or physical symptoms in the absence of mood and/or anxious symptoms is not sufficient for a diagnosis. In the majority of cases, at least five of the following symptoms must be present in the week before the period, start to improve within a few days after the onset, and become minimal in the week following:

- Depressed mood;
- Anger or irritability;
- Trouble concentrating;
- Lack of interest in activities once enjoyed;
- Moodiness;
- Increased appetite;
- Insomnia or the need for more sleep;
- Feeling overwhelmed or out of control;
- Other physical symptoms, the most common being belly bloating, breast tenderness, and headache;
- Symptoms that disturb your ability to function in social, work, or other situations;
- Symptoms that are not related to, or exaggerated by, another medical condition.

Causes of PMDD: In 2017, researchers at the National Institutes of Health (NIH) found that women with PMDD are more sensitive to changes in the sex hormones estrogen and progesterone, and they found that this might be due to a molecular mechanism in their genes. Researchers compared white blood cells in women with PMDD and those without and confirmed that women with PMDD had differences in the genes that process sex hormones.

Risk Factors:

- **Environmental:** Stress, history of interpersonal trauma, and seasonal changes are all environmental factors associated with the presence of premenstrual dysphoric disorder.

- **Genetic:** While the heritability of premenstrual dysphoric disorder is unknown, it is estimated that premenstrual symptoms generally are 50% heritable.

- **Menstrual Cycle Modifiers**: According to the DSM-5, women who use oral contraceptives may have fewer premenstrual complaints than do women who do not use oral contraceptives.

PMDD Treatment:

Medication: A group of antidepressants named selective serotonin reuptake inhibitors (SSRIs) can be prescribed to women suffering from PMDD. Moreover, over-the-counter pain relievers may help with breast tenderness, muscle aches and pains, cramps, and headaches.

Birth Control: In 2010, the FDA

approved the birth control pill containing drospirenone and Ethinyl estradiol to treat PMDD. It may be worth talking to your doctor or gynaecologist to determine whether or not this birth control pill is right for your body and could help with your PMDD symptoms.

Nutritional supplements: Consuming 1,200 milligrams of dietary and supplemental calcium daily may possibly reduce symptoms of PMS and PMDD in some women. Vitamin B-6, magnesium and L-tryptophan also may help, but talk with your doctor for advice before taking any supplements.

Herbal remedies: Some research suggests that chasteberry (Vitex agnus-castus) may possibly reduce irritability, mood swings, breast tenderness, swelling, cramps and food cravings associated with

PMDD, but more research is needed.

Diet and lifestyle changes: Regular exercise often reduces premenstrual symptoms. Cutting back caffeine, avoiding alcohol and stopping smoking may ease symptoms, too. Getting enough sleep and using relaxation techniques, such as mindfulness, meditation and yoga, also may help. Avoid stressful and emotional triggers, such as arguments over financial issues or relationship problems, whenever possible.

Psychotherapy: Living with severe depression and anxiety shouldn't be something you have to face alone. Cognitive behavioural therapy (CBT) is a structured, action-oriented type of psychological treatment that focuses on the interaction between thoughts, feelings, and behaviours. CBT has been shown to be an effective treatment for mood and anxiety disorders and has also been shown to help people cope better with physical symptoms, such as pain.

Situational depression

Situational depression is a short-term, stress-related type of depression. It can develop after you experience a traumatic event or series of events. Situational depression is a type of adjustment disorder. It can make it hard for you to adjust to your everyday life following a traumatic event. It's also known as reactive depression.

Symptoms can include:
- listlessness;
- feelings of hopelessness and sadness;
- sleeping difficulties;
- frequent episodes of crying;
- unfocused anxiety and worry;
- loss of concentration;
- withdrawal from normal activities as well as from family and friends;

- suicidal thoughts.

After a difficult life event, whether it is a change in a relationship, the loss of your job, or the death of a loved one, the stress of the situation can cause you to feel sad, helpless, apathetic, lost, irritable, or even hopeless. You might cry frequently, feel listless and unable to focus or find yourself unable to cope with normal, day-to-day tasks. Things you are normally able to handle seem overwhelming or impossible. Most people who experience situational depression begin to have symptoms within 90 days of the triggering event.

According to the DSM-5, to be **diagnosed** with situational depression, you must:

- Begin experiencing symptoms within three months of the stressful event or series of events;

- Have symptoms that cause marked distress and significantly interfere with daily life;
- Have symptoms that are not the result of another condition or related to substance or alcohol use;
- Have symptoms that are not a normal part of the grieving process after the death of a loved one.

Causes: Situational depression begins after some sort of major life change or trauma. Some of the events that may trigger the onset of this form of depression include:

- Death of a loved one;
- Divorce;
- Relationship problems;
- Relocating;
- Job loss;
- Financial problems;
- Illness;

- Unstable employment;
- Unstable living situation;
- Retirement;
- Serious accidents;
- Natural disasters;
- Social issues at home, school, or work.

Certain factors may increase the risk of situational depression. These include:

- Having an existing mental health condition;
- Past childhood stress and trauma;
- Experiencing multiple traumas or stressors at the same time;
- A family history of depression.

Treatment:

Psychotherapy is the preferred method of treatment for situational depression and can help a person to understand and process how a stressor has impacted their lives. Therapy can help a person to problem-solve and provide them with healthy coping skills, interventions, and techniques. Support groups may also be recommended for a person struggling with situational depression, as extra support and validation can be received from others who are experiencing similar challenges.

Antidepressants are not typically used in the treatment of adjustment disorder with depressed mood. While medications may provide some symptomatic relief, treatment usually involves addressing the underlying problems and stressors that are contributing to the symptoms.

Once treatment is helping you address your depression, you can also make some **lifestyle changes** that can help you cope.

These include:
- getting exercise;
- establishing healthy sleeping habits;
- getting more rest and relaxation;
- eating more healthfully;
- strengthening your social support system.

Self-care and Self-Help

There are some things people can do to help reduce the symptoms of depression. For many people, regular exercise helps create a positive feeling and improve mood. Getting enough quality sleep regularly, eating a healthy diet and avoiding alcohol can also help reduce symptoms of depression. When you're depressed, it can feel like there's no light at the end of the tunnel. But there are many things you can do to lift and stabilize your mood. The key is to start with a few small goals and slowly build from there, trying to do a little more each day. Feeling better takes time, but you can get there by making positive choices for yourself. If left untreated, depression and anxiety can go on for months, even years. The good news is that a range of effective treatments are available, as well as things you can do yourself to recover and stay well. You might like to try a few of the following ideas for lifestyle changes and social support. Most people find that a combination of things works best. It's important to remember that recovery can take time, and just as no two people are the same, neither are their recoveries. Be patient and go easy on yourself.

Healthy lifestyle

Staying well is about finding a balance that works for you, but there are some general principles that most people find useful. These include maintaining a healthy lifestyle – eating a healthy, balanced diet; doing some form of regular physical activity; and having a good night's sleep. It can also be useful to cut back on alcohol and drugs. Reducing and managing your stress levels by making sure that you make time to do something distracting, relaxing, satisfying or enjoyable each day – even if you initially feel you can't be bothered – can also help. You may find it helps to get the help of a friend or family member to help you stay active. It's also important to deal with any setbacks and keep trying. **Regular exercise** can be as effective as antidepressant medication in countering the symptoms of depression. Take a short walk or put some music on and dance around. Start with small activities and build up from there. **Increase mood-enhancing nutrients** such as Omega-3 fatty acids. Some people use natural remedies, such as herbal medicines, to treat mild-to-moderate depression like: **St. John's wort** (This is not suitable for people who have or may have bipolar disorder), **Ginseng** (Practitioners of traditional medicine may use this to improve mental clarity and reduce stress), **Chamomile** (This contains flavonoids that may have an antidepressant effect), **Lavender** (This may help reduce anxiety and insomnia). Some supplements may also help treat these symptoms like: **S-adenosyl methionine (SAMe)** and **5-hydroxytryptophan** (this may help boost serotonin, the neurotransmitter in the brain that affects a person's mood). Results of a 2019 study suggest that a **diet** rich in fruits, vegetables, fish and olive oil helped reduce depression symptoms. **Aerobic exercise** raises endorphin levels and stimulates the neurotransmitter norepinephrine, which is linked with mood. This may help relieve mild depression. **It is essential to speak to a doctor before using any type of herbal remedy or supplement to treat depression. Some herbs can interfere with the action of drugs or otherwise make symptoms worse!**

Learning about your condition

As with any health condition, the more you learn and know about depression and anxiety conditions, the better able you will be to work out what's right for you. It's important to learn the facts using reliable sources of information. It may be worth talking to your doctor or mental health professional about what you've read if you want to make sure it is accurate and reliable.

Support Groups

Support groups for people with depression and anxiety can provide an opportunity to connect with others, share experiences and find new ways to deal with challenges from others who have experienced the same issues as you. Contact your local community health centre or the mental health association/foundation in your state or territory to find your nearest group, or try searching online. Some people prefer to seek and offer support or share their stories via online forums.

Relaxing Training

Relaxation training calms your body and mind, which in turn helps to reduce anxious thoughts and behaviour. It may also help you feel more in control of your anxiety. There are several different types of relaxation training, such as breathing exercises that teach you how to slow down and regulate your breathing, or progressive muscle relaxation which teaches you to relax by learning how to tense and then relax specific groups of muscles. Another type of relaxation training involves thinking of relaxing scenes or places. Relaxation training can be learned from a professional or done by yourself.

Family, Friends and Nature

The people close to you can play an

important role in your recovery by providing support, understanding and help, or just being there to listen. It can be hard to socialise if you're experiencing anxiety or depression, and many people tend to withdraw or avoid social contact. But spending time alone can make you feel lonelier and cut off from the world, which in turn makes it harder to recover. It is important to try to get out and spend time with your family and friends and keep saying 'yes' to social invitations – even if it's the last thing you feel like doing. It can help to talk about how you are feeling with someone who is caring and supportive. Even if you are not looking for support, it can still be helpful to let family and friends know what you are going through, so they are aware. This can help them to support you better. If you don't feel like talking and interacting, try an activity where you don't have to make conversation, like watching a movie or playing sport. Staying connected improves your wellbeing and confidence, and doing some physical activity has the added bonus of helping you keep fit and bust stress. Spend some time in nature, care for a pet, volunteer, pick up a hobby you used to enjoy (or take up a new one). The simple act of talking to someone face-to-face about how you feel can be an enormous help. The person you talk to doesn't have to be able to fix you. They just need to be a good listener—someone who'll listen attentively without being distracted or judging you.

According to National Institute of Mental Health: As you continue treatment, you may start to feel better gradually. Remember that if you are taking an antidepressant, it may take 2 to 4 weeks to start working. Try to do things that you used to enjoy. Go easy on yourself. Other

things that may help include:
- Trying to be active and exercise;
- Breaking up large tasks into small ones, set priorities, and do what you can as you can;
- Spending time with other people and confide in a trusted friend or relative;
- Avoiding self-medication with alcohol or with drugs not prescribed for you;
- Set realistic goals for yourself;
- Try to spend time with other people and confide in a trusted friend or relative;
- Try not to isolate yourself, and let others help you;
- Expect your mood to improve gradually, not immediately;
- Postpone important decisions, such as getting married or divorced, or changing jobs until you feel better.

Discuss decisions with others who know you well and have a more objective view of your situation;

- Continue to educate yourself about depression.

How can I help a loved one who is depressed?

If you know someone who has depression, first help him or her see a health care provider or mental health professional. You can also:

- Offer support, understanding, patience, and encouragement;
- Never ignore comments about suicide, and report them to your loved one's health care provider or therapist;
- Invite him or her out for walks, outings, and other activities;
- Help him or her adhere to the

treatment plan, such as setting reminders to take prescribed medications;

- Help him or her by ensuring that he or she has transportation to therapy appointments;
- Remind him or her that, with time and treatment, the depression will lift.

Treatment

Depression, even the most severe cases, can be treated. Between 80 percent and 90 percent of people with depression eventually respond well to treatment. Almost all patients gain some relief from their symptoms. The earlier that treatment can begin, the more effective it is. Depression is usually treated with medications, psychotherapy, or a combination of the two. If these treatments do not reduce symptoms, electroconvulsive therapy (ECT) and other brain stimulation therapies may be options to explore. Before a diagnosis or treatment, a health professional should conduct a thorough diagnostic evaluation, including an interview and possibly a physical examination. In some cases, a blood test might be done to make sure the depression is not due to a medical condition like a thyroid problem. The evaluation is to identify specific symptoms, medical and family history, cultural factors and environmental factors to arrive at a diagnosis and plan a course of action.

Medication

Brain chemistry may contribute to an individual's depression and may factor into their treatment. For this reason, antidepressants might be prescribed to help modify one's brain chemistry. They may help improve the way your brain uses certain chemicals that control mood or stress. You may need to try several different antidepressant medicines before finding the one that improves your symptoms and has manageable side effects. A medication that has helped you or a close family member in the past will often be considered. Antidepressants may produce some improvement within the first week or two of use. Full benefits may not be seen for two to three months. Psychiatrists usually recommend that patients continue to take medication for six or more months after symptoms have improved. Longer-term maintenance treatment may be suggested to decrease the risk of future episodes for certain people at high risk. There are many different types of antidepressant medication which have been shown to work, but their effectiveness differs from person to person. Antidepressants can make you feel better, but they won't change your personality or make you feel happy all the time.

If a patient feels little or no improvement after several weeks, his or her psychiatrist can alter the dose of the medication or add or substitute another antidepressant. In some situations, other psychotropic medications may be helpful. It is important to let your doctor know if a medication does not work or if you experience side effects. Although antidepressants can be effective for many people, they may present serious risks to some, especially children, teens, and young adults. Antidepressants may cause some people, especially those who become agitated when they first start taking the medication and before it begins to work, to have suicidal thoughts or make suicide attempts. Anyone taking antidepressants should be monitored closely, especially when they first start taking them. For most people, though, the risks of untreated depression far outweigh those of antidepressant medications when they are used under a doctor's careful supervision. In some cases, children, teenagers, and young adults under 25 may experience an increase in suicidal thoughts or behaviour when taking antidepressants, especially in the first few weeks after starting or when the dose is changed. This warning from the U.S. Food and Drug Administration (FDA) also says that patients of all ages taking antidepressants should be watched closely, especially during the first few weeks of treatment. Like taking any other medication, some people will experience some side effects, and individuals should discuss the risks and benefits with their doctor. People should also ask for information about the medications so that they can make an informed decision. Depending on which medication is taken, common side effects can include nausea, headaches, anxiety, sweating, dizziness, agitation, weight gain, dry mouth and sexual difficulties (e.g. difficulty becoming/staying aroused). Some of these symptoms can be short-lived, but people who experience any of these symptoms should tell their doctor, as there are ways of minimising them. The likelihood of a particular side effect happening varies between individuals and medications.

Stopping antidepressant medication should only be done gradually, on a doctor's recommendation and under supervision.

Types of antidepressants:

Selective Serotonin Reuptake Inhibitors (SSRIs)

This class includes sertraline; citalopram; escitalopram; paroxetine; fluoxetine; fluvoxamine. SSRIs are:

- maybe the most commonly prescribed antidepressants;

- often a doctor's first choice for most types of depression;

- generally well tolerated by most people;

- generally non-sedating.

Serotonin and Noradrenalin Reuptake Inhibitors (SNRIs)

This class includes venlafaxine; desvenlafaxine; duloxetine. SNRIs:

- have fewer side effects compared to the older antidepressants;

- are often prescribed for severe depression;

- are safer if a person overdoses.

Reversible Inhibitors of MonoAmine oxidase (RIMAs)

The class includes the moclobemide. RIMAs:

- have fewer side effects;

- are non-sedating;

- may be less effective in treating more severe forms of depression than other antidepressants;

- are helpful for people who are experiencing anxiety or sleeping difficulties.

TriCyclic Antidepressants (TCAs)

The class includes nortriptyline; clomipramine; dothiepin; imipramine; amitriptyline. TCAs are:

- effective, but have more harmful side effects than newer drugs (i.e. SSRIs);

- more likely to cause low blood pressure – so this should be monitored by a doctor.

Noradrenaline-Serotonin Specific Antidepressants (NaSSAs)

This class includes mirtazapine. NaSSAs are:

- relatively new antidepressants;

- helpful when there are problems with anxiety or sleeping;

- generally low in sexual side effects, but may cause weight gain.

Noradrenalin Reuptake Inhibitors (NARIs)

This class includes reboxetine. NARIs are:

- designed to act selectively on one type of brain chemical – noradrenaline;

- less likely to cause sleepiness or drowsiness than some other antidepressants and more likely to:

- make it difficult for people to sleep;
- cause increased sweating after the initial doses;
- cause sexual difficulties after the initial doses;
- cause difficulty urinating after the initial doses;
- cause increased heart rate after the initial doses.

Monoamine Oxidase Inhibitors (MAOIs)

This class includes tranylcypromine. MAOIs are prescribed only under exceptional circumstances as they require a special diet and have adverse effects.

Psychotherapy

Psychotherapy, or "talk therapy," is sometimes used alone for treatment of mild depression; for moderate to severe depression, psychotherapy is often used in along with antidepressant medications. There are several types of effective psychological treatments for depression, as well as different delivery options. Some people prefer to work one on one with a professional, while others get more out of a group environment. A growing number of online programs, or e-therapies, are also available. Psychotherapy may involve only the individual, but it can include others. For example, family or couples therapy can help address issues within these close relationships. Group therapy involves people with similar illnesses. Depending on the severity of the depression, treatment can take a few weeks or much longer. In many cases, significant improvement can be made in 10 to 15 sessions. Psychological treatments can help you change your thinking patterns and improve your coping skills so you're better equipped to deal with life's stresses and conflicts. As well as supporting your recovery, psychological therapies can also help you stay well by identifying and changing unhelpful thoughts and behaviour. Psychotherapy helps by teaching new ways of thinking and behaving, and changing habits that may be contributing to depression. Therapy can help you understand and work through difficult relationships or situations that may be causing your depression or making it worse. Effective treatment for depression often includes consulting a therapist who can provide you with tools to treat depression from a variety of angles and motivate you to take the action necessary. Therapy can also offer you the skills and insight to prevent depression from coming back.

Cognitive behavioural therapy (CBT) has been found to be effective in treating depression. **Cognitive behaviour therapy** is a structured psychological treatment which recognises that the way we think (cognition) and act (behaviour) affects the way we feel. CBT is one of the most effective treatments for depression and has been found to be useful for a wide range of ages, including children, adolescents, adults and older people. CBT involves working with a professional (therapist) to identify thought and behaviour patterns that are either making you more likely to become depressed, or stopping you from getting better when you're experiencing depression. It works to change your thoughts and behaviour by teaching you to think rationally about common difficulties, helping you to shift negative or unhelpful thought patterns and reactions to a more realistic, positive and problem-solving approach. CBT is also well-suited to being delivered electronically (often called e-therapies). A person may have CBT in individual sessions with a therapist, in groups, over the telephone, or online.

Interpersonal therapy (IPT): IPT is a structured psychological therapy that focuses on problems in personal relationships and the skills needed to deal with these. IPT is based on the idea that relationship problems can have a significant effect on someone experiencing depression, and can even contribute to the cause. IPT helps you recognise patterns in your relationships that make you more vulnerable to depression. Identifying these patterns means you can focus on improving relationships, coping with grief and finding new ways to get along with others. Interpersonal therapy aims to help people identify:

- emotional problems that affect

relationships and communication;

- how these issues also affect their mood;
- how all of this may be changed.

Behaviour therapy: While behaviour therapy is a major component of cognitive behaviour therapy (CBT), unlike CBT it doesn't attempt to change beliefs and attitudes. Instead, it focuses on encouraging activities that are rewarding, pleasant or satisfying, aiming to reverse the patterns of avoidance, withdrawal and inactivity that make depression worse.

Mindfulness-based cognitive therapy (MBCT): MBCT is generally delivered in groups and involves a type of meditation called 'mindfulness meditation'. This teaches you to focus on the present moment – just noticing whatever you're experiencing, whether it's pleasant or unpleasant – without trying to change it. At first, this approach is used to focus on physical sensations (like breathing) but then moves on to feelings and thoughts. MBCT can help to stop your mind wandering off into thoughts about the future or the past, and avoid unpleasant thoughts and feelings. This is thought to be helpful in preventing depression from returning because it encourages you to notice feelings of sadness and negative thinking patterns early on before they become fixed. As a result, you're able to deal with warning signs earlier and more effectively.

Electroconvulsive Therapy

Electroconvulsive Therapy (ECT) is a medical treatment most commonly used for patients with severe major depression or bipolar disorder who have not responded to other treatments. ECT is the best-studied brain stimulation therapy and has the longest history of use. It involves a brief electrical stimulation of the brain while the patient is under anaesthesia. A patient typically receives ECT two to three times a week for a total of six to 12 treatments. ECT has been used since the 1940s, and many years of research have led to major improvements. It is usually managed by a team of trained medical professionals including a psychiatrist, an anesthesiologist and a nurse or physician assistant. This may be effective if psychosis occurs with depression. If medications do not reduce the symptoms of depression, electroconvulsive therapy (ECT) may be an option to explore. Based on the latest research:

- ECT can provide relief for people with severe depression who have not been able to feel better with other treatments.

- Electroconvulsive therapy can be an effective treatment for depression. In some severe cases where a rapid response is necessary or medications cannot be used safely, ECT can even be a first-line intervention.

- Once strictly an inpatient procedure, today ECT is often performed on an outpatient basis. The treatment consists of a series of sessions, typically three times a week, for two to four weeks.

- ECT may cause some side effects, including confusion, disorientation, and memory loss. Usually, these side effects are short-term, but sometimes memory problems can linger, especially for the months around the time of the treatment course. Advances in ECT devices and methods have made modern ECT safe and effective for the vast majority of patients. Talk to your doctor and make sure you understand the potential benefits and risks of the treatment before giving your informed consent to undergoing ECT.

- ECT is not painful, and you cannot feel the electrical impulses. Before ECT begins, a patient is put under brief anaesthesia and given a muscle relaxant. Within one hour after the treatment session, which takes only a few minutes, the patient is awake and alert.

Other more recently introduced types of brain stimulation therapies used to treat medicine-resistant depression include repetitive transcranial magnetic stimulation (rTMS) and vagus nerve stimulation

(VNS). Other types of brain stimulation treatments are under study.

Final Words

Thanks to everyone who was interested in this book. I hope each of you has been able to bring out the needed knowledge so that you can help both yourself and the people you love.